GREG DAVIS

eCOMMERCE HANDBOOK

Boosting Your Profits with eCommerce

GREG DAVIS

GREG DAVIS

ISBN: 1517142148
ISBN-13: 978-1517142148

DEDICATION

This book is dedicated to all the
Artrepreneurs out there trying to make
the world a bolder place with their art.

GREG DAVIS

CONTENTS

GREG DAVIS

ACKNOWLEDGMENTS

My first job in eCommerce marketing was working for a Russian family in New Jersey. They hired me because they needed someone who could help market their eCommerce store using American speak or lingo to which they didn't possess. That rare opportunity introduced me to a new wild west, eCommerce.

Although the eCommerce industry has become far more common place than it was over a decade ago when I worked in my first store, it remains the wild west and a great place for niche products and services.

I've had the fortunate opportunity to work amongst several brilliant people, from marketers, to designers, to programmers. I write this book while standing on the shoulders of giants.

Special Thanks to Brian Ross and Mike Hollos, the best eCommerce developers on the planet!

Special Thanks to Connie Pheiff, Olga Gikas and Emily Fritz for coaching, editing and wordsmithing this book.

FOREWARD

Every so often, someone encapsulates a timely idea in such a striking book that the idea quickly penetrates the general consciousness. Such is the case with this book, Greg Davis' groundbreaking work, his first book. I feel so privileged to be invited to write this Foreword.

Greg Davis is an epochal figure in his own time, and remains one, for that matter. He creates a "new approach" across the newer field of "Artrepreneur." You can agree or disagree on his writings, but Greg Davis is offering you something achievable ~ profitability! Just like every artist and entrepreneur, knowingly or not, pays his dues and one way or another, become disciples of Greg Davis.

When I say that
Boosting Your Profits with eCommerce
creates a "new approach," I'm serious. This book, more than any other book on artistic profitability, will alter your entire concept of reaching your dreams with a new paradigm that stresses human potential and human behavior. Greg never succeeded in keeping his feet on the desk, he knows what it takes to help you achieve your dreams.

- Connie Pheiff, Primetime Radio Host
Chairwoman & CEO PHEIFFacademy

AUTHOR'S NOTE

It doesn't matter if you're a musician, a painter, a performer, a jeweler; I wrote this book to educate and empower artrepreneurs to inject eCommerce into their business strategy. eCommerce continues to be a growing industry that can be launched out of a small apartment with the scalability of growing into an eCommerce conglomerate.

There is nothing comforting about the idea of being a "starving artist". You shouldn't settle for waiting to be discovered or "chosen." You are the verb; you drive the action that dictates your career, and that's where eCommerce comes into play.

As a strategic management coach for artrepreneurs with over 25 years of sales and marketing experience, including a decade of eCommerce and digital marketing effectiveness, I can tell you that eCommerce can catapult your profits and make you the envy of your peers.

Although I coach individuals and corporations on creating winning business strategies, this book is not as much about strategy as it is an eCommerce 101 instruction book that will teach you the fundamentals of creating your own eCommerce business, including:
- Registering your domain name; how and why
- Choosing an eCommerce store platform
- Defining multichannel digital marketing
- Working with website developers

This book will educate and break down some of the technology barriers that scare artrepreneurs into starting an online business.

If you're interested in starting your own business or are simply looking for incremental revenue; Boosting Your Profits with eCommerce will guide you into the world of eCommerce & online marketing and empower you to make wiser choices from the start, so you can avoid costly mistakes.

If you have a product or service you can sell in person or over the phone, you can sell it online. I'll show you how...

Quotes

"Here's to the crazy ones, the misfits, the rebels, the troublemakers, the round pegs in the square holes... The ones who see things differently — they're not fond of rules... You can quote them, disagree with them, glorify or vilify them, but the only thing you can't do is ignore them because they change things... They push the human race forward, and while some may see them as the crazy ones, we see genius, because the ones who are crazy enough to think that they can change the world, are the ones who do."
  - *Steve Jobs*

"Times and conditions change so rapidly that we must keep our aim constantly focused on the future."
  - *Walt Disney*

"Without deviations from the norm, progress is not possible"
  - *Frank Zappa*

"If someone likes you, they'll buy what you're selling, whether or not they need it."
  - *Gene Simmons*

"The music that really turns me on is either running toward God or away from God. Both recognize the pivot, that God is at the center of the jaunt."
  - *Bono*

"Be who you are and say what you feel, because those who mind don't matter, and those who matter, don't mind."
  - *Dr. Suess*

"I suck at being normal"
  - *Greg Davis*

INTRODUCTION

You're about to enter an exciting industry where the only constant is that things change constantly. You will reach buyers around the world. You will gain loyal customers who will develop a one-on-one relationship with you and your business. You will be an artrepreneur with scalability and the opportunity to generate a profitable business with your passion.

I have two professional passions in my life; music and eCommerce. The first I was born with; the latter grew out of the wild success I've witnessed and helped develop in the eCommerce industry.

I think my passion for eCommerce comes from my desire to do bold things and to have a non-traditional career. eCommerce, is the new wild west where individuals could venture online and strike gold. Who isn't inspired, motivated or jealous when hearing about a company that launched a store or an app and sold it for millions of dollars? Although the Mark Zuckerberg and Steve Jobs' stories are inspiring, I'm only partly motivated by their story. They are one-in-a-million success stories with talent, tech savvy, business acumen and a lot of fortunate encounters.

No, what gets me excited about eCommerce and digital marketing is the retired doctor selling his recommended vitamins online; the stonecutter selling pet memorials across the country; the bored executive selling model planes to other enthusiasts. It's those people that get me excited about digital marketing and eCommerce, because they're everyday people capable of creating a global business for themselves without being computer gurus or wealthy.

I'm not a tech guy. I'm a marketer, a strategic manager and an artist. However, the way I grow profits for myself and my clients is by leveraging digital strategies through eCommerce. Often, when I tell people I work in digital marketing or eCommerce, they ask me questions about fixing their computer. I'm not that guy and I cannot help them. So, I write this with the fullest sincerity that if I can make it online, anyone can.

It's like driving a car. I can jump in a car or on a motorcycle and I can control that vehicle. However, that's where my car expertise ends (aside from pumping gas and changing a tire). Even though I can't build a car, can't repair a car, it doesn't stop me from controlling the destination of this large machine. That's eCommerce! You don't need to know how to build it learn how to drive the results you want.

Get ready to reach an international audience with your 24/7/365 sales person. It all starts with a click...

1

A BUSINESS IS A BUSINESS

Before you get starry-eyed and shop for your own island with the profits from your online business, let me caution you with a simple fact. A business is a business is a business. I don't care if you're running a brick and mortar business or an online store. It's still a business; and to be successful you have to treat it with the respect of a business.

I've had many experiences with clients who believe they'll launch a website today and sales will start rolling in without anything more to the site. Sorry; that's not the way it goes. If you're looking for easy money, try a government handout.

Launching an eCommerce or online business is a lot of work, but it offers several benefits and advantages, including:
1. You need very little startup costs and overhead
2. You don't need to own product to start
3. You can compete in a global marketplace

The beauty of eCommerce is that it's the great commerce equalizer. If you're a brick and mortar, you can't begin to compete with Nike, Target or Sears. However, online, your picnic table could be in the same search results as Sears or your sports clothing could beat Nike's listing without needing the same budget they do on branding.

When shopping online, it's products, keywords and price that drive the sale. Use that to your advantage.

Questions to ask yourself

Before you get started, there are a couple of questions you need to ask yourself…

1. Why am I starting an online business?
2. Am I willing to challenge myself to learn new technology?
3. Am I prepared to invest time and money to see this business succeed?

Even though you can start and succeed online with smaller budgets, you should also consider how much you believe in your business idea. If you had a big budget, would you launch the same business? Don't start an online business just because it's cheap. Start the business you'd love to have, but do it online because it's cheaper and can provide better return-on-investment (ROI).

2

DEFINING THE INDUSTRY

eCommerce is defined as merchants transacting business online either by business-to-business (B2B) or business-to-consumer (B2C).

eCommerce's roots can be traced back to 1979, when Michael Aldrich invented online shopping, and 1981, when Thomson Holidays conducted the first true online order. However, eCommerce didn't evolve from a novelty concept into an industry until 1991, when the World-Wide-Web (www.) launched. In 1995, when Amazon.com went live, commerce was forever changed.

I always say, if there's a good or service you can sell to your neighbor, you can sell it to the world online. The industry includes traditional goods and services, but is not limited to product and services such as:

- Banking
- Consumer
- Education
- Engineering
- Energy
- Oil and Gas
- Fast-Moving Consumer Goods (FMCG)
- Financial (Finance)
- Food and beverage
- Government

- Healthcare
- Insurance
- Manufacturing
- Media
- Real estate
- Religion
- Retail
- Technology
- Telecommunications
- Transportation (Travel)

The Top 5 performing industries in eCommerce include:
1.   Books and Magazines
2.   Computer Software
3.   Sports and Fitness
4.   Jewelry and Watches
5.   Video Games

Questions to ask yourself

1.   What types of products could I sell online?
2.   Do I want to sell in my town, nationwide, worldwide?
3.   Do I have a product that would have international appeal?

You want to be sure you're passionate about the products or services you decide to sell online. Just because a particular product may sell well, you shouldn't sell it without having a deep interest in that product. Sell what you know and love, and it will show in how your customers interact with your website and brand. Niche websites (websites that provide specific information or products to a target audience) perform very well in eCommerce. Don't be afraid to do something niche to a smaller target audience, because with enough passion and dedication, you may just corner that   market.

3

THE WONDERFUL WORLD OF BUZZWORDS

Spend a day at a marketing or ad agency and you'll be immersed in acronyms and buzzwords. Everything from getting a drink of water to launching a giant advertising campaign in Times Square seems to have a buzzword attached to it. Sometimes it's necessary, because who wants to say 'search engine optimization' all the time when you can just say SEO? However, don't let yourself be intimidated by the buzzwords.

Below is a glossary of eCommerce and digital marketing terms. Have fun throwing them around at your next dinner party.

Affiliate marketing or performance marketing is a pay-per-acquisition marketing tactic where a merchant will work with an affiliate network to make discount offers available to blogs and coupon sites. When someone uses a coupon or discount from a particular "affiliate," that affiliate earns a referral commission paid to them via the affiliate network.

Comparison Shopping Engines (CSE) are shopping search engines that allow a user to compare prices across multiple online stores.

Email marketing leverages subscribers to your website or blog as a database of potential buyers. Using an Email Service Provider (ESP) merchants will email offers and newsletters to subscribers.

Keywords are specific words that relate to your products or industry. Keywords drive search engine results. A user types in a keyword of something they're looking for and, based on relevancy, websites will show up that relate to that keyword.

META tags or META descriptions are HTML tags that provide details about a Web page. They do not affect how the page displays to users; their main purpose is to provide Web page information to search engines.

Organic traffic is the term describes search engine traffic that is driven to your site based on the content you have created, not paid advertising. If a user does a search for 'carpet cleaning supplies' and you sell makeup, you won't be found in those search results. But if you do sell those products, your website may show up in the listings of that search query.

Payment gateway is a service that sends credit card transactions/information to credit card payment networks for processing. It is required in order for you to accept credit card payments through your store. It is the online equivalent of a point-of-sale (POS) system used in a brick and mortar business.

Pay-Per-Click (PPC) also known as cost-per-click (CPC) is an advertising tactic where merchants bid on keywords or phrases to get better placement in paid search results in a search engine. The cost per keyword the merchant pays is based on the number of clicks on their ads that send users to their websites.

Responsive design (or adaptive design) is when your website's design automatically dynamically resizes and adapts to the size of any device screen, (i.e. Desktop, Tablet, Smartphones, Laptops). The key difference in responsive design vs. non-responsive design is that a non-responsive website will stay full-width but shrink to fit into a screen of a mobile device, for example, making your content small and difficult to read or take action. Responsive design will reshape your content, so that it is easy to read on any device.

Return-on-Investment (ROI) is the profit gained from investing in a business or marketing campaign.

SEO (Search Engine Optimization) is the phrase which describes the process by which your website is "optimized" so it can rank favorably in 'organic listings', the data people see when they search for information or products using a search engine like Google or Bing. For example, when

you search for 'carpet cleaning supplies in Cincinnati,' a list of websites is shown. This is different than 'paid ads' that will be seen in the same area.

Social media marketing is a form of marketing that involves using social media platforms (i.e. Facebook, Twitter, LinkedIn, Instagram, Google+, etc.) to build brand recognition and advocacy for your brand.

Title tags are seen in the title of your webpage or website. They are used primarily to create keyword relevance for your particular Web page, based on your keyword terms. Users and search engine "spiders" (a program that visits your page to assess its content) see this information.

Website hosting is a service that enables your website to be available on the Internet. Your website is code, a hosting service sends that code live to the Internet.

4

THE ANATOMY OF A WEBSITE

A big frustration you could encounter in talking to technical people about the specifics of your website is not understanding the anatomy of your website. Remember, this is your 365/24/7 salesperson and you need to know how it ticks.

Below are the basic terms that describe the anatomy of your website and how they're used.

Header (see Figure 1): This is found at the top of your website where your logo and other contact information typically go. The header is static (unchanged) in that it will remain the same for anyone browsing your website.

Figure 1

Body (see Figure 2): This is the content area of your website. It will contain the information about you and your business. What the information within the body contains is dependent on the page the user is on.

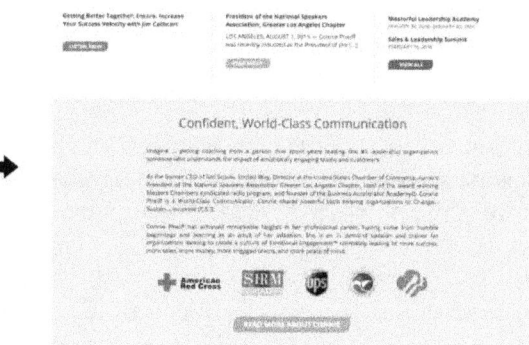

Figure 2

Footer (see Figure 3): The footer is typically where you'll find copyright information or badges, as well as links that may direct a user to information that are not product-specific and don't fit in your website's primary navigation. Footer links can serve a positive SEO purpose to your website. Don't think that just because it's the bottom of your website that search engines don't care…they do.

Figure 3

Call to Action (See Figure 4): A Call to Action (CTA) is your website's way of asking for the sale. You want to make sure your website is always inviting people to learn more or take an action. CTA phrases like "Get Started", "Learn More" or "Contact Us" are common and effective call to action terms to use on your website.

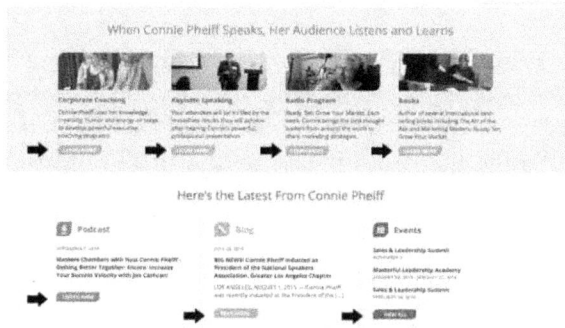

Figure 4

To see a live example, visit: www.conniepheiffspeaks.com.

5

SHOPPING CART PLATFORMS

A shopping cart platform is the engine that will drive your online sales transactions. Informational websites are websites that simply list information about a product or business and typically the only transaction that will occur is a user completing a contact form, or signing up to a mailing list.

In eCommerce, it's all about making money. Your website requires the ability to make a sales transaction. A shopping cart platform for your website is the way that happens.

There are several shopping cart platforms available for small- to medium-sized business that will include not only the ability to transact sales but will also serve as your website, which is what you want. Don't use an informational website and then slap a "shop" button on it sending people to a different URL.

The exception to this is if the majority of your website content is already built to so serve as an informational website. You want to do everything you can to keep people on your website. It's better for SEO and a better user experience for your customers.

The following is a short list of reputable Do-It-Yourself (DIY) eCommerce website platforms:

Illuminate: http://yahoo.smallbusiness.com

Shopify: www.shopify.com

3dcart: www.3dcart.com

Bigcommerce: www.bigcommerce.com

Volusion: www.volusion.com

Woo Commerce (WordPress): www.woocommerce.com

eBay Stores: http://stores.ebay.com/

Amazon Webstore: http://webstore.amazon.com/

If you're looking to work with a cart geared toward medium- or enterprise-sized eCommerce stores, consider the following word of caution. If you're new to eCommerce, stick with the SMB (small- and medium-sized business) shopping cart platforms.

AspDotNet Storefront: www.aspdotnetstorefront.com

Magento: www.magento.com

NOTE: Many eCommerce shopping cart platforms have partnership with DOBA (Dropshipper). This will make it easier for you to integrate your products with a few clicks.

DOBA: www.doba.com

6

MULTICHANNEL MARKETING STRATEGIES 101

At this point, I need to bring you into the weeds a bit to explain to you what multichannel marketing strategies mean and how they're leveraged for driving sales through your website.

First, let's look at how people can find your website:

Search Traffic: They click on a link to your website from the search results page on a search engine and can either be organic (natural listings) or paid traffic (from online search ads).

Direct Traffic: They know the name of your website (e.g., www.mybusiness.com) and go directly to your site.

Referral Traffic: They click a link on another website that directs them to a page on yours.

To increase traffic to your site, you have to let people know it exists through marketing efforts.

Email Marketing: Recruit email subscribers to your newsletter. Typically, you will acquire these subscribers via your website or through an online email signup form. You can also use offline methods to collect emails from interested people. **NOTE:** NEVER purchase an email list. It's a waste of money and bad practice. If you're using an Email Service Provider (ESP) for your email marketing, they will most likely shut your account down for using a purchased list. I've seen it, so just don't use it.

The best practice is to get people to opt-into your email list and let it grow naturally.

Blog Post: Blogs are an excellent source of generating new content online that can help you improve your search engine rankings.

Press Release: Press releases are great for media coverage, but they're also a good source for generating SEO and referral traffic by linking your online press kit to your website and/or by the mention of your domain name in the press release. If many online publishers pick up your story, it's a natural way to grow your list of linking domains, which is a signal to search engines that your website is credible.

Social Media: Social is a strong source for generating traffic to your site, but be careful not to oversell on social. Promote, advocate, network on social, but don't expect sales from social. Also, some social networks, like Facebook, have strict guidelines for soliciting on their networks, so make sure you verify that the content you are adding follows those guidelines.

Each of these are effective marketing channels. A singular path could lead a user to your website. When you use more than one of these channels, you are creating a "multichannel marketing campaign".

You don't have to use all of them when you're just starting out (in fact, that isn't recommended), but you should know they're available to you, and once you can leverage them effectively, your business will soar.

7

MULTICHANNEL MARKETING STRATEGIES 102

Let's take a look at how these multichannel marketing campaigns can work together to promote your store.

SCENARIO 1

Step 1: A user is looking for a bicycle helmet. She goes to Google and types in 'bicycle helmets'.

Step 2: Through the organic results, she sees a list of companies selling bicycle helmets. One of those stores is yours. She clicks on the link for www.mybusiness.com.

She has just reached your business via an organic search engine result.

Step 3: She browses your website, but doesn't buy anything yet. However, she sees your mailing list link and signs up to receive future offers.

Step 4: You have a sale on Friday and send an email to everyone who has subscribed on your mailing list. She receives the email and clicks on your email link sending her back to your store.

Step 5: She searches for a coupon code on affiliate websites and finds a "10% off" coupon.

Step 6: She makes a purchase on your website and shares a post on

Facebook and Twitter letting her friends and followers know about the great deal she just got.

SCENARIO II

Step 1: Your business sends out a press release.

Step 2: Your release is shared on social media

Step 3: Users read about your business and type in www.mybusiness.com. Other users click on the online version of your press release and are directed to your website.

Step 4: A blogger reads about you and writes an article about you or your products and links to your website. Readers of that blog see your story and click on blog article to visit your website.

Step 5: Users signup on your mailing list and shop for products.

Now, this is a simplified example, but it's a realistic scenario of what it means to effectively leverage a multichannel marketing strategy to drive sales for your business.

8

EARN MONEY IN YOUR SLEEP

Recurring revenue is probably the single most important term you want to keep top of mind as you strive to create a profitable business. It is expensive and time-consuming to get new customers or clients. You spend a considerable amount of time and money networking, marketing, advertising and more. However, when you can earn a customer or client that will pay you on a regular basis, you can begin to project your revenue each month. You truly begin to build profitability, because you're spending as much time earning new customers to pay the bills and because you can count on the recurring paying customers/clients you have.

Easier said than done, but possible, very possible. You need to develop some revenue streams by leveraging your website.

Aside from selling products online, you can also earn commissions simply by recommending products in your blog or by adding a badge to your website. This is largely referred to as Affiliate Marketing or Performance Marketing.

Here's how it works:

A brand offers an affiliate program. You sign up as an affiliate and receive a percentage of a sale from that company. You list their logo with a link to their site, or simply a link to a particular product. That link is traced specifically to you with what's referred to as a "Pixel". When a user on your website clicks on that link, they are directed to that brand's website. If they make a purchase, you receive the credit for that sale and earn a commission.

Affiliate marketing is a multi-billion dollar industry and, rest assured, there are several artrepreneurs out there making their living on affiliate marketing alone.

As a band, you should create an affiliate program for your products. It will help motivate your fans to promote your band by letting them earn money for raving about you if people buy your merchandise from their referral.

Question to ask yourself

• What could I do to create recurring revenue?

9

GETTING STARTED

Let's talk about the basics of getting your eCommerce store launched. Here's a simple checklist of things you'll need in order to get open for business.

1. Registering a Domain: Your domain name is the name of your website (e.g., AcmeCarpetCleaning). You'll need to have a top level domain name (TLD). TLDs are the part of the domain name located to the right of the dot (" . "). The most common TLD's are .com, .net and .org. Names get harder and harder because there are so many domain names purchased already.

It's a profitable business for people to purchase domain names to resell to corporations and individuals willing to pay a premium to acquire a particular domain name. Most eCommerce platforms have a built in domain registrar tool you can use when signing up for our store. You can also use a platform such as GoDaddy to register your domains.

Your domain registration DOES NOT need to be from the shopping cart you use. You may need to get creative with your URL, but remember someone needs to type your domain name if they want to go directly to it in the future. www.mybusiness.com is an easy 2 word domain name to use. www.ritascoolbusinessname.com is a bit more challenging. Also, remember, people make typos, so consider buying incorrect spelling of your domain name to ensure your competitors don't capitalize on clumsy fingers.

2.   Choosing a Shopping Cart Platform: When you choose the eCommerce shopping cart platform you want to go with, you'll simply register your business name with them and then you will be walked through the set-up of your store. Most have a design theme you can start with and if you want something more personalized, you can work with custom website developers.

Be careful that you have solidified your business name before signing up for your store. The reason to be careful is that your customer receipts, your confirmation emails, every communication you have, will list that store name. If you sign up for www.mybusiness.com and then decide you want it to be www.mysweetbusiness.com, you'll have to jump through several hoops in order to have that id changed with your store platform. Save yourself the trouble and make certain that you know the name you want to use when signing up for an shopping cart account.

3.   Getting Products: Don't have a product of your own?   No problem, use a drop shipper. Using a drop shipper involves signing up with a service that carries a wide variety of products that will ship to your customers on your behalf. You simply sign up with them (some fees typically apply) and gain access to thousands of products you can add to your store including images, descriptions and pricing. You'll have to work with the margins for your profitability.

4.   Payment Processing: You need a bank to accept the financial transactions of your store. You'll want to work with a merchant account services provider or payment processor. Nearly all, if not all shopping cart platforms allow you to integrate with PayPal to accept payments. It's a quick and easy setup; however, PayPal has steeper fees than other banks and so if you want to save money on transaction fees, especially if you find yourself doing high volume, find a merchant account services provider who can provide you with a customized solution at more competitive rates.

5.   Setup Taxes: You're going to be working with a global or at least a national customer base. You'll want to make sure your store is set up to apply taxes where applicable. Most shopping carts have built in widgets to help you with this setup.

10

BEWARE OF THE SHARKS

The Internet has created second and third careers for many people. Not only for the eCommerce merchants that are making sales online, but also services professionals with expertise in the industry. There are copywriters, programmers, designers, marketers, analytics gurus, product developers... a wide field of experts, ready to help you grow your business. However, like any industry, there are also some sharks out there looking for a quick buck to burn you.

Here are some tips on things to watch out for when seeking a reputable vendor to help you with your eCommerce store.

The SEO guru: Watch out for promises to be #1 on Google. Although it is possible to reach #1 on Google, you shouldn't buy a promise from anyone that they'll get you there. There's no magic formula for SEO, it's a series of several steps coming together to work for you. Plus, Google and the other search engines frequently change their algorithms, just to keep it interesting.

Here's a simple trick that someone can use to get you #1 on Google. They'll use an obscure keyword that would be unique or rarely used by any shoppers out there looking for your product. For example, if you're selling bicycle helmets, you will want to use search terms that mom, dad, and bicyclist will be typing into Google to find a product to buy. That will make it harder to get to #1 because there's more competition, but it's more honest and it can happen with enough effort around a particular keyword strategy.

Scope Creep: Take time to scope your project. Many website developers out there want to give you a website both you and they can be proud of. However, pride can be subjective. If you're not a developer, you typically don't know all of the capabilities of a website. There are many things that are considered table stakes and other things you need that might be more custom. That's where scoping out a project is key.

Your job as an eCommerce merchant is to learn how to make your buyer's experience as appealing as possible, so they'll be a repeat customer and buy more from you. To build that experience, you may need to work with a website developer. The worst thing that can happen to you and your developer is to buy/sell a website project and find out it doesn't do what you need it to do. If this happens, it's not the developer's fault, it's yours. The developer works with lots of merchants who all have different needs. It's your job to effectively communicate your site's objective to your developer. If you don't do that, it's your loss. Therefore, explain to your developer the experience you want your customers to have. Let the developer then come back to you with a quote on how to make that possible. Don't just keep throwing good money after bad and complain that your developer needs more money to do what you asked for. If you need help finding a developer and aren't sure what to look for, call me, I'll help you.

You get what you pay for: You ever see those ads on TV about how you can get your website for only $10.00 a month or even better FREE? Always remember that you get what you pay for. Imagine walking into a mall and wanting to lease store space. If they told you it was FREE or $10.00 a month, what do you think you would get? A leaky storage closet with maybe some mice or rats and an unknown odor that won't leave. Now, what exactly do you think you'll get for FREE or $10.00 when you launch your website? Make a real investment into your profitability by choosing a reputable developer that expects more from you but will give you more in return.

11

BEWARE OF YOURSELF

Your business goal should be to create a profitable business with something you're passionate about. Remember, this is an investment of your time and money, so don't go for the easy sale. Leverage your passion to fill the world with your products.

Don't be afraid to ask for help with this. The biggest concern I have for Do-It-Yourself businesses is that you can easily find the passion for your craft, and not have enough passion left over to become an eCommerce, SEO or email marketing expert to further your business goals. However, if you are going to ask for help, ask for the right help from the right people. Don't ask your friends or family, unless they can benefit in some way from offering their assistance. Mom, Dad, and Cousin Barney may mean well, but they have bills to pay, too.

If you ask for help, treat it as a joint venture, so that others have something to gain for their time.

This book is created to serve as a basic background in eCommerce websites and marketing strategies, but if you need to be coached on these subjects, find a mentor, attend workshops or seminars on the subject matter.

ABOUT THE AUTHOR

Strategy Coach, podcaster, musicians, marketer and author, Greg Davis is an inspirational thought leader and one of the most sought after and unconventional keynote artists in the industry. Drawing from his success as a musical Artrepreneur, Greg is a master at increasing productivity and profitability by inspiring teams and individuals to become possibility thinkers and virtuoso performers. As a change-agent, Greg will embrace your dreams and develop strategic steps that transform you and your team from thinking like a garage band to performing like rock stars ready to headline Madison Square Gardens.

An award-winning eCommerce marketing leader, Greg has generated millions of dollars for eCommerce merchants in varying product verticals. His professional portfolio includes several small to medium sized eCommerce merchants and such notable brands as eBay Inc. and Web.com.

Looking for a Strategy Coach
to increase your productivity and profitability?

CONTACT GREG

EMAIL: INFO@RHYTHMOFPROFITABILITY.COM

WWW.RHYTHMOFPROFITABILITY.COM

LOOKING FOR A DYNAMIC
AND ENTERTAINING SPEAKER?

Greg Davis is the authority on creating a profitable Artrepreneurial business.

Greg is often referred to as a "practical poet" for his down to earth storytelling. His lessons of Musical Artrepreneurship is uplifting and motivating audiences across the country. Artists, musicians, business leaders, event planners, universities, associations and artrepreneurs in need of awaking their inner rock star, should call Greg.

His most requested keynote topics are:
• Your Business is Like a Band
• Building Your Business's Marketing Platform
• The Manager's Song: Overcoming the challenges of first-time managers
• Give First, Give Fast, Give Often: Leveraging eCommerce for Nonprofit Fundraising

CONTACT GREG

EMAIL: INFO@RHYTHMOFPROFITABILITY.COM

WWW.RHYTHMOFPROFITABILITY.COM

ARE YOU IN NEED OF ECOMMERCE DEVELOPMENT AND CREATIVE SERVICES?

Greg Davis is an award-winning eCommerce marketer with over a decade of eCommerce and digital marketing expertise. Greg will help you develop a profitable eCommerce strategy and will help you assemble a team full of the best of the best in eCommerce website design, digital marketing and custom programming to make your eCommerce business thrive.

CONTACT GREG

EMAIL: INFO@RHYTHMOFPROFITABILITY.COM

WWW.RHYTHMOFPROFITABILITY.COM

www.ingramcontent.com/pod-product-compliance
Lightning Source LLC
Chambersburg PA
CBHW070233210526
45168CB00020B/2146